MW01602994

LifeBook

The Authority, Authenticity and
Accuracy of God's Word

GRAHAM

P.O. Box 799070
Dallas, TX 75379
1-800-414-7693 (1-800-414-POWER)
jgraham@powerpoint.org
jackgraham.org

L

R ECENTLY I VISITED with a woman who was facing the
end of the earthly road we walk. Despite the uncertainty and
perplexed emotions that accompany imminent death, she seemed
strangely serene and completely devoid of fear. I asked about
her confidence, her optimistic outlook, her undeniable sense of
peace; in reply she said, "I'm resting in the Word of God."

God's comforting holy Word—I think you'd agree there is
no better book to die by.

I contend there's also no better look for *life*. True, if the
Bible isn't sure, if it isn't settled, then any old book will do. But it
is sure. It *is* settled. And it ushers in strength for today. There is
only one book in existence that points us to life and love in Jesus
Christ, and that book is God's great Word.

An episode of *Larry King Live* recently featured a
five-member panel made up of ministers who were giving their
thoughts on the subject of God and war. While I think it is completely appropriate for Christians to respond to the issues of war
and peace in our times, I believe those responses must be rooted
in something other than personal opinion or political preference.
I was amazed as I listened to several from that panel express
individual beliefs that had no basis whatsoever in the Bible.
In all of life, in fact, we must ask the question, *How does the Word*

of God come to bear on this issue? Every ethical quandary is solved in the Source of Truth, and thankfully, God himself has written those solutions down.

> I go to the Word of God when I face the imponderables and "unexplainables" that creep in from time to time.

I go to the Word of God when I face the imponderables and "unexplainables" that creep in from time to time. When there's war, when there's death, when there's tragedy, when there's cancer in a child, when there's an accident and we don't understand, where do we go? We go to God and to his Word.

In the Gospel of John, we read that many of Jesus' disciples deserted him along the way because they found "followership" a bit too tough. As they walked away from him, Jesus looked at the twelve disciples who knew him best and said, "Do you want to go away as well?"[1]

According to John 6:68-69, Simon Peter was the one to answer on their behalf: "Lord, to whom shall we go? You have the words of eternal life, and we have believed, and have come to know, that you are the Holy One of God." Jesus does possess the words of eternal life, the words that are always full of power,

---

[1] John 6:67. [All Scripture references are from the ESV unless otherwise noted.]

full of relevance, full of the wisdom we need in order to enjoy our God-given purpose in this world.

One of the best things I did as a young Christian was to begin to memorize Scripture. Not only did the practice help to keep me far from sin, but it also cleansed me from the sin I did happen to discover. I've been studying, pondering, and reflecting on God's Word for many decades now, and my hope is that I will always crave this marvelous Book of Life. After all, it's the *truth* that transforms. It's the *truth* that alters attitudes. It's the *truth* that hijacks bad habits and evicts errant ways. It's the *truth* that introduces insight and brings grace and peace to life. It's the *truth*—about heaven and hell, life and death, right and wrong, joy and sorrow, wrongdoing and forgiveness—that gives meaning to our minutes and makes sense of the sum total of our days.

I remember reading one time that the great evangelist Billy Graham once struggled with the veracity of Scripture. He'd seen several of his classmates abandon their belief in the Bible as God's infallible Word and wrestled with whether his faith was also misplaced. Recalling those wobbly and wavering days, Graham said this:

I believe it is not possible to understand everything in the Bible intellectually. One day some years ago I decided to accept the Scriptures by faith. There were problems I could not reason through. When I accepted the Bible as the authoritative Word of God by faith I found immediately that it became a flame in my hand. That flame began to melt away unbelief in the hearts of many people and to move them to the side for Christ. The Word became a hammer breaking up stony hearts and shaping men into the likeness of God. Did God say, "I will make my words in my mouth like fire, and is not my word like a fire," and, saith the Lord, "like a hammer that breaketh the rocks to pieces?"

I found that I could take a simple outline and put a number of Scripture quotations under each point and God would use it mightily to cause men to make a full commitment to Christ. I found that I did not have to rely upon cleverness, or oratory, or psychological manipulation, apt illustrations or striking quotations from famous men. I began to rely more and more upon the Scripture itself and God blessed it, and I am convinced through my travels and experience that people all over the world are hungry to hear the Word of God.[2]

---

[2] *www.graceefc.com/yteaching/bgrahambibleauthority.doc*.

Whether we sense it viscerally or not, I believe every person on the planet indeed is hungry to hear the Word of God. We long for our mouths to be controlled, for our hearts to become more compassionate, for our lives to somehow count. But we're not sure how to get there. We don't know where to turn.

I believe every person on the planet indeed is hungry to hear the Word of God.

But there God stands, ready to intervene, anxious to enhance our appreciation and comprehension of his inspired, inerrant Word, his Holy Scripture—the Bible, the *LifeBook* on which we can lean.

WHAT IS THE BIBLE?

Every summer Americans celebrate the birthday of our nation. And if you paid attention in sixth-grade history class you'll recall that the United States has a *constitutional* form of government. After long and rigorous debate, the framers and the founders of this nation drafted and delivered to us a Constitution that was presented to representatives of thirteen federated states and then ratified as the official law of the land.

The presupposition of our Constitution is this: *the law is absolute.* In other words, we are to be a nation not of leaders, but of laws. As a result, citizens of this nation have always been free to

pursue the life of their choosing, as long as those pursuits fall within the laws of the land. Throughout this country's history great prosperity has been brought to its people, and many would contend that that good fortune is due solely to the good form of government we've observed.

> **The Bible is the highest law of God and therefore is the ultimate authority for all of life.**

Similarly, just as the Constitution of the United States is the foundation upon which this society rests, the Word of God—the Bible—(perhaps in a more noble and eternal sense) is the "Constitution" of the Christian faith. The Bible is the highest law of God and therefore is the ultimate authority for all of life. So, just where did this "law of God" come from? Let's keep going.

In his book *Evidence that Demands a Verdict*, author and apologist Josh McDowell lists the various facts that figure into the origin of the Bible:

◊ The Bible was written over a 1,500-year span which covered more than forty human generations.
◊ The Bible was written by more than forty different authors

from every walk of life: variously they were fishermen, farmers, poets, preachers, shepherds, kings, tax collectors, scholars, military leaders, doctors, political officials, and more.

◊ The Bible was written in a host of places on three different continents, including Asia, Africa, and Europe.

◊ The Bible was written in three languages—Hebrew, Aramaic, and Greek—and from numerous perspectives, including history, law, poetry, didactic treatises, parable and allegory, biography, personal letters, memoirs, and prophecy.

◊ The Bible covers a multitude of subjects, many of which are considered controversial.

Yet with all this diversity included in its composition, each part of the Bible contributes individually to one unfolding story: God's marvelous redemption of humankind.

What an incredible idea to ponder, that a lengthy book could be written without collaboration by more than forty authors over a millennium and a half and could reflect a single theme and common agreement, down to the most minute details! The obvious truth is that there has never been another book like the Bible, and there can be no accounting for the origin and perpetuity of the Bible outside of supernatural means.

The historical accuracy, the geographical accuracy of Scripture, the fulfilled prophecies, the textual criticism or studies of the text, the preservation of the biblical text including both Old Testament and New Testament—there are many reasons to trust in the infallibility of God's Word. The Bible is the most scrutinized book in all of the world and yet no ancient manuscript of any kind contains the kind of preservation and integrity that the Bible itself possesses.

The Bible is an infallible ancient text. It is the inspired Word of God. It is necessary doctrine, that, according to self-testimony in 2 Timothy 3:16, is useful for "teaching, for reproof, for correction, and for training in righteousness." God's Word not only restores our spiritual strength and sets our feet on the right path once more, but also helps to keep us there, on the course marked out for maturity.

WHAT GOD SAYS ABOUT HIS INSPIRED WORD

Knowing how the Bible came into existence is one thing; understanding *why* it's here is another matter altogether! Perhaps no clearer word of Scripture can be found that concerns the distinctiveness and purposefulness of God's words to humankind than Isaiah 55:8-11. In that passage we read this: "For my thoughts are not your thoughts, neither are your ways my ways, declares the LORD. For as the heavens are higher than the earth, so are my ways higher than your ways and my thoughts than your thoughts.

"For as the rain and the snow come down from heaven and do not return there but water the earth, making it bring forth and sprout, giving seed to the sower and bread to the eater, so shall my word be that goes out from my mouth; it shall not return to me empty, but it shall accomplish that which I purpose, and shall succeed in the thing for which I sent it."

> **Truly we would be without knowledge of our Creator unless he came to us speaking our language.**

Notice two things which are stated clearly in this passage. First, *the thoughts of God are different from the thoughts of human beings*. To oversimplify, it's like a person who speaks only English being in the same room with a person who speaks only Mandarin Chinese. There can be precious little verbal communication unless one learns the language of the other. In our case, it was an impossible proposition for humankind to learn the language of God, since God is "other" than humankind. Truly we would be without knowledge of our Creator unless he came to us speaking *our* language, which is precisely what he did. The Bible clearly reflects the initiative that God took on our behalf as he reached out to communicate with humankind at different times throughout history. Hebrews 1:1-2 says, "Long ago, at many times and in many ways, God spoke to our fathers by the prophets, but in these last days he has spoken to us by his Son, whom he appointed the heir of all things, through whom also he created the world."

Without question, it was elating for the people who heard God speak firsthand at those "various times," but what about the revelation of God's will for successive generations, including ours? God moved men to record a portion of what he spoke "at various times and in various ways" for the benefit of *all* people, regardless when they would live. Because God's words are not our words, he put his words into a permanent format by which they could be apprehended and applied throughout history and for the benefit of every man, woman, and child who would be born on planet Earth.

Second, *God's words have purpose.* God does not send forth his words arbitrarily, capriciously, or carelessly. *Every* word that God speaks has a purpose in his overall plan, and therefore every word comes to us via his inspiration and direction. Our lack of agreement with or our misunderstanding of God's sentiments does not change the conditions under which those sentiments are deployed!

When I consider God's spoken Word, forever documented in the Bible, I think of a trumpeter at our church who often accompanies Prestonwood's choir during Sunday morning Worship Services named Larry Brubaker. Just as Larry's breath exhales melodic notes, God too sounded a clear signal every time he "played" a series of written notes. And just as Larry arranged various notes to form a unified tune, God arranged the lives, personalities, attitudes, and capacity for understanding of each biblical author so that the end result would be sweet to the reader's ear. As a musician brings his horn to life by blowing into it, so God animated the authors of Scripture by breathing inspiration into and then through them, thereby conveying his message of redemption and grace to the sum of humankind. But there is more. Not only did God the Father testify to the truth of his Word, but so too did the person of Jesus Christ.

WHAT JESUS CHRIST SAYS ABOUT SCRIPTURE

Whether it is a company, a church, a service organization, a club, or a family, the flow of values and beliefs from the organization's leaders to its members ultimately determines the level of cohesiveness, harmony, and productivity.

In the Church of Jesus Christ, there is no debate or discussion about who is the "head" of the Church. Jesus is our Lord, and we are the members of his body—the living, growing organism we call the Church. His teachings, not to mention the firsthand example of his life, form the foundation upon which we live. He is the Vine, and we are the branches; he is the Head, and we are the parts; he is the Master, and we are

> **We are the members of his body – the living, growing organism we call the Church.**

the servants—about his role in his Church, there is little debate.

For instance, when was the last time your church debated whether or not we as Christ's followers should love one another? When was the last time there was an all-church meeting to decide whether we should practice forgiveness? What about patience or peace, or whether we are to take up our cross and follow Christ? We adhere to these values because our Leader, through his life experience and through the everlasting Word of God, has taught us to prize them.

To the latter, in one passage of Scripture, found in Matthew 5:17-19, we find a concise outline that reflects Jesus' perspective on that powerful Word of God. By his own testimony he reveals that Scripture is *authoritative* (verse 17), *authentic* (verse 18), and *accurate* (verse 19). If we will adopt his perspective on the Bible, as we do on the other central tenets of the Christian faith like reflecting love and patience and peace, then the Bible battles will cease, battles over whether the Word of God is inspired, whether it is true, whether it is complete, and whether it is to be taken as inerrant fact ... or as nothing more than fantasy. Only then can we as believers rightly devote all of our attention and resources to spreading the Gospel and ministering to the needs of a hurting world.

THE AUTHORITY OF THE BIBLE

To the casual reader of the four Gospels, it could be easy to overlook that Jesus Christ knew the Old Testament Scriptures from start to finish, and this despite not one mention of his having a copy of the Law, Prophets, or Writings as he traveled through-out the land of Israel. Indeed, he *couldn't* have had a personal copy much as we have our own copy of the Bible today because copies of Scripture were kept only in the synagogues. And yet the words of the Old Testament flowed from his lips with clarity and ease as he spoke. From his youngest years to adulthood, Jesus must have

devoted significant time to the study and memorization of the Old
Testament; we do well to remind ourselves when reading the four
Gospels that when Jesus makes reference to or quotes the Old
Testament, he is doing it spontaneously and from memory.

From the beginning to the end of his life, Jesus' attitude
toward the Word of God was one of submission to its authority.
As a twelve-year-old boy, he astounded the scribes—the teachers
of the Law—in the temple courts, both by his questions and his
answers concerning the things of God[3]. At the outset of his public
ministry, Jesus was led by the Spirit into a conflict with Satan
himself. Jesus resisted all of Satan's temptations by submitting
to the authority of the Word: "It is written ... it is written ... it is
said...," says Luke 4:4, 8, 12. "It is written"—or its counterpart,
"that the Scripture might be fulfilled"—became the phrase the
disciples heard more than any other, such as is reflected in the
following verses:

◊ Then Jesus said to them, "You will all fall away because
of me this night. For it is written, 'I will strike the
shepherd, and the sheep of the flock will be scattered.'"
–Matthew 26:31

---

[3] See Luke 2:41-52.

◊ For the Son of Man goes as it is written of him, but woe to that man by whom the Son of Man is betrayed! It would have been better for that man if he had not been born. –Mark 14:21

◊ For I tell you that this Scripture must be fulfilled in me: "And he was numbered with the transgressors." For what is written about me has its fulfillment. –Luke 22:37

◊ I am not speaking of all of you; I know whom I have chosen. But the Scripture will be fulfilled, "He who ate my bread has lifted his heel against me." –John 13:18

◊ While I was with them, I kept them in your name, which you have given me. I have guarded them, and not one of them has been lost except the son of destruction, that the Scripture might be fulfilled. –John 17:12

Shortly after Jesus' temptations-in-the desert experience, in a synagogue in Nazareth, he revealed himself as the Messiah or the "anointed one" to the Jewish leaders by reading and then applying to himself the Messianic passage from Isaiah 61:1-2, also cited in Luke 4:14-21. Admittedly he could have saved himself a measure of trouble by sitting quietly in the synagogue instead of acknowledging that he, in fact, was the long-awaited One.

Whatever the cost, he knew he had to obey the Word and teach what was true.

Finally, he revealed that his earthly mission included suffering and even death, his reference point always including Old Testament prophecies concerning the suffering Messiah.

As a relatively young man in his early thirties, humanly speaking, Jesus maintained an astounding grasp of the Word of God and remained totally submissive to its authority.

Throughout his life, Christ seemed to be committed to two things: the will of his Father in heaven, and the authority of Scripture. And yet he saw them as somehow inseparable. His submission to the authority of Scripture was the way he *demonstrated* his submission to his Father. In Matthew 5:17, Jesus says, "Do not think that I have come to abolish the Law or the Prophets; I have not come to abolish them but to fulfill them." He fulfilled what was written in Scripture with the same fidelity with which he fulfilled what his Father in heaven commanded him to do. The Father's words, whether given to him directly or written in the pages of the Old Testament, were the *authoritative Word of God*. Jesus understood that, "Forever, O LORD, your word is firmly fixed in the heavens," as Psalm 119:89 declares. The Word and will of God is (present tense) settled forever; therefore, Jesus never questioned it. Anyone who is a follower of Jesus Christ can rest assured in the very same claim.

THE AUTHENTICITY OF THE BIBLE

Not only did Jesus testify to the authority of Scripture, but also he testified to its *authenticity*. Jesus viewed Scripture as being verbally inspired by God. When he read the Old Testament scrolls— whether the Law, the Prophets, or the Writings, which includes the Psalms and the wisdom literature such as the book of Proverbs, he read confidently, believing that he was reading the *authentic words given by God to man*. Matthew 5:18 says, "For assuredly, I say to you, till heaven and earth pass away, one jot or one tittle will by no means pass from the law till all is fulfilled" (NKJV).

The word "jot" is an English rendering of the Greek word for *iota*, the ninth letter of the Greek alphabet, translated by our English letter "i." This Greek word was used to approximate the smallest letter in the Hebrew alphabet, the *yodh*, which is similar to our apostrophe ('). "Tittle" is a translation of Greek *keraia* ("horn") and refers to a small stroke of the writing pen used to make an accent mark, or to complete a serif on the end of a letter. So, Jesus said, not even the smallest mark of the pen will go unnoticed in the fulfillment of the Law. *Every* word, *every* letter, *every* stroke of the pen that records the Word of God matters.

All of Scripture, in other words, was authentically inspired by God.

Was Jesus using hyperbole for effect? Certainly. But it was exaggeration toward a critical point: Everything that God has revealed to humankind is important. None of it is extraneous or unnecessary.

> **Every word, every letter, every stroke of the pen that records the Word of God matters.**

This can be a tough concept for modern people like you and me to swallow because we're so accustomed to weeding through extraneous and unnecessary information on a moment-by-moment basis. It seems we're constantly exposed to stuff we don't really need to know—in newspapers, in magazines, in books we read for pleasure, on billboards we pass as we face our morning commute—and so as we approach the holy Word of God, we tend to think that surely there must be irrelevant things there too. Like the rest of what we read in life, we think the Bible is nice, but unnecessary; interesting, but optional; enjoyable, but peripheral to the "real stuff" of life.

These assumptions couldn't be further from the truth.

I'm so thankful for a pastor who instilled in me early in my

Christian life a rock-solid confidence in God's Word. Year by year, I would learn to trust more and more in the infallibility of the Bible, finding not hidden flaws but hidden wonders and hidden excellencies that further revealed the majesty of God.

When I was in my early thirties, my confidence in God's Word would be put to the test. At the time, I was the pastor of First Baptist Church in West Palm Beach, and suddenly I found myself in a meeting with other leaders from my denomination, where the topic of discussion was whether or not the Bible is inerrant. Imagine my surprise: I didn't know the subject was up for debate!

One by one, the moderator asked us to share our positions on this issue, and I was shocked and saddened as I absorbed opening comments from many of my peers. They had doubts, they said, about the trustworthiness of the Bible.

I began to have doubts about *them*.

It was almost my turn when I felt a surge of anxiety rush through my system. What was I going to say?

When all eyes at last were on me, I decided to keep it simple—and true. "The Bible is the Word of God," I said, and then repeated: "The *Bible* is the *Word of God*."

All was silent as my words hung in the air, but then the

pastor sitting next to me piped up: "You mean the Bible *contains* the *words* of God," he said.

I couldn't believe my ears. "No, that's not what I mean. What I *mean* is that the Bible *is* the Word of God."

There is a subtle but strong difference between those two beliefs—does the Bible merely contain some of God's words, or is the Bible the Word of God? In neo-orthodox, existential styles of biblical understanding and interpretation, the belief that the Bible contains the words of God centers on the Bible as a vehicle for God's truth instead of centering on the Bible as God's truth itself. It focuses on various parts and parcels of the Bible being true, instead of focusing on the entirety of God's Worth as Truth.

But this belief doesn't square with the apostle Paul's validation in 2 Timothy that we looked at earlier, which says that "all Scripture is breathed out by God..."[4] *Every* word of God is pure. And *every* word of God is true. The Bible is the inerrant Word of God.

THE ACCURACY OF THE BIBLE

The third testimony from Jesus' words in Matthew 5 says this: "Therefore whoever relaxes one of the least of these commandments and teaches others to do the same will be called least in

[4] 2 Timothy 3:16a.

the kingdom of heaven, but whoever does them and teaches them will be called great in the kingdom of heaven" (verse 19). In other words, Jesus' expectation of his followers is that we would honor the accuracy and importance of every single commandment offered in Scripture, and that we would teach others to do the same.

In our culture today, great weight is placed on the "biggest and the best." Some is good, more is better, and all is best. The smaller something is, the less significance it carries—in our carnal eyes, at least. The bigger it is, the more important it must be. The biggest car, the biggest house, the biggest following, the biggest resume, the biggest bank account— the biggest people are the ones more worthy of our attention and admiration.

Jesus' expectation of his followers is that we would honor the accuracy and importance of every single commandment offered in Scripture.

But this is the exact opposite of Jesus' position in Matthew 5.

According to Jesus Christ, nothing could be further from the truth. Jesus believed that the Scriptures are *accurate*, not just in the broad strokes of history, but down to the minutest detail—things like the tenses of verbs and whether a noun is singular or plural. Both in ancient times and still today, it's Jesus' example that Bible students follow when they learn to study the Bible in the original Hebrew, Aramaic, and Greek languages. Precise grammatical form was used to write the Bible, and it's critical that those who want to learn from Scripture learn Scripture as it was originally written.

There are many other evidences of Jesus' confidence in the accuracy of Scripture. For example:

◊ He believed Adam and Eve were literal people (Matthew 19:4).

◊ He believed the story of Jonah and the great fish was a literal occurrence (Matthew 12:40).

◊ He believed that Daniel the prophet wrote the book of Daniel (Matthew 24:15).

◊ He believed that Noah, the ark, and the flood happened just as Genesis says it did (Matthew 24:37-38).

◊ He believed that Sodom [and Gomorrah] were literal cities that were buried under fire and brimstone from heaven (Luke 17:29).

God is in the details just as much as he is in the broad brushstrokes of life.

Why was Jesus confident appealing to things like grammar and to biblical history to convey truth? Because he knew that the tenses of verbs and the numbers of nouns and the records of history in the Bible were inspired by God. He knew that God is in the details just as much as he is in the broad brushstrokes of life.

You and I have a choice to make, based on three options that exist: We will choose to believe that there are errors in the Bible that Jesus was unaware of, which would mean that he wasn't all-knowing in the end; we will choose to believe that there are errors in the Bible—stories, fables, and legends that Jesus *did* know about but didn't bother to tell *us* about, which would make his testimony one plagued with dishonesty; or we will choose to believe that the Bible indeed is the Word of God and that it is 100 percent accurate, without any mixture of error, just as Jesus testified. May you and I wisely choose the third option, every day of our lives.

WHAT OUR LIVES SAY ABOUT THE BIBLE

It's not only by God the Father and God the Son that we receive testimony regarding the truth of the Bible; by God's Spirit, *anyone* who has experienced the power of the Word of God in his or her life can give testimony to the fact that the Bible is not just another book.

Hebrews 4:12 says that the Word of God is alive, far more than dried ink on old paper. It is "living and active, sharper than any two-edged sword, piercing to the division of soul and of spirit, of joints and of marrow, and discerning the thoughts and intentions of the heart." In other words, the Bible is a book to be *demonstrated*, not *debated*. Because the Word of God is alive, you and I can have a *fresh encounter* each time we approach it. Reading, studying, and living in the truths of the Word of God is unlike engaging with any other book on earth. When was the last time a history book saved your marriage, healed your wounded spirit, encouraged your teenage child, corrected a sinful habit in your life, or gave you courage and hope in the face of disease, despair, or even death? Unlike another known book, people who embrace and consume the Word of God will be *changed*.

They may be healed (Psalm 107:20).
They may be convicted of sin (2 Timothy 3:16).
They may be born again (1 Peter 1:23).
They may receive faith (Romans 10:17).
They may increase in holiness (Ephesians 5:26)
They may be able to resist Satan
(Ephesians 6:17).
They may be able to resist sin (Psalm 119:9).
They may become fruitful and strong (Psalm 1:3).
They may have their life changed in an
infinite number of ways.

All because the Bible is not just a book, but is the living Word of God given to save us and make us whole.

If you want to be blessed in your life—beautifully and powerfully blessed—then look to the Word of God, listen to the Word of God, and live the Word of God. Approach it as you would a relationship with a good friend—expectantly, enthusiastically, energetically, and excitedly. You never know what you might discover or what God will supernaturally reveal to you when you open the marvelous pages of his Word! The Bible is an inexhaustible storehouse of spiritual riches, wisdom, counsel, and truth. And it's yours to consume today.

Ж

Since the days when I was a little boy sitting on my grandfather's knee, it has been my desire to know and live by the Word of God. Grandpa Sims would read various Bible stories out loud, and my young ears knew even then that those utterances were more than average words. They were *special* words—words of life.

It would take many years for my young mind to mature and

to grasp more fully how truly set apart is God's Word, and with each step of that journey I have found myself more fulfilled, not less. I pray you'll take the next step on that journey too, beginning with adopting the following four views as your own:

View the Bible as authoritative, submitting yourself to it without reservation. Come with questions if need be, but stay until you allow God to answer them. John 7:17 says, "If anyone's will is to do God's will, he will know whether the teaching is from God...". Trust God to reveal his unique voice to you through his Word.

If God inspired any of the Bible, then he inspired all of it.

View the Bible as authentic, remembering that if God inspired any of the Bible, then he inspired all of it. Each time you approach the Bible, ask God to show you what he would like for you to learn from the passage you are reading. In the well-written words of Psalm 119:18, ask God, "Open my eyes, that I may behold wondrous things out of your law."

View the Bible as accurate, believing that if Jesus Christ trusted in the accuracy of all that is written in the Bible, we may too. Rest assured that the Bible can withstand your scrutiny. Be like the Bereans of old who studied the Scriptures daily to verify the accuracy of what the apostle Paul was teaching them.[5] If you find something you don't understand or can't resolve, get help from your pastor or from a good Bible study resource. Keep in mind that just as the earth reveals its gold and silver treasures to the diligent, according to Proverbs 2:3-5, so does the Word of God.

View yourself as a "welcomer of the Word." Make it a lifelong quest to prove to yourself what an amazing book the Bible is. In James 1:21 we read: "Therefore put away all filthiness and rampant wickedness and receive with meekness the implanted word, which is able to save your souls." We are humbly to welcome the Word because it is by the Word—God's truth—that we are made free. Some are in bondage, some have errant habits, some have addictions, and those in these chains wonder why. Jesus said in John 8:32, "You will know the truth, and the truth will set you free." It is only by truth that we become free.

))(

---

[5] See Acts 17:11.

I've never been much for working in the yard. My wife, Deb, will be the first to tell you! In fact, our son Jason, who is married and has a yard that he is very proud of, is gifted at landscaping in ways that defy his genetics. The other day his wife, Toby, told me that Jason had on his hat and his work clothes and his gloves, and as he reached for his wheelbarrow en route to the yard he said, "I'm about to go where no Graham male has ever gone before." So I'm not an expert on the whole sowing-and-reaping thing, but I do know that if you're going to grow a decent lawn, you first have to get the weeds out. This simple principle is one of God's favorite descriptions of his Word—that it is a seed in the hearts of every man and woman alive.

In Matthew 13 Jesus tells a powerful parable, known as the Parable of the Sower to many people. Verses 1-9 read as follows:

That same day Jesus went out of the house and sat beside the sea. And great crowds gathered about him, so that he got into a boat and sat down. And the whole crowd stood on the beach. And he told them many things in parables, saying: "A sower went out to sow. And as he sowed, some seeds fell along the path, and the birds came and devoured them. Other seeds fell on rocky ground, where they did not have much soil, and immediately they sprang up, since they had no depth of soil, but when the sun rose they were scorched. And since they had no root, they withered away. Other seeds fell among thorns, and the thorns grew up and choked them. Other seeds fell on good soil and produced grain, some a hundredfold, some sixty, some thirty. He who has ears, let him hear."

It's a dangerous thing to hear the Word of God, a dangerously marvelous thing.

A seed produces life and fruit, and so does the Word of God, which is why Jesus says, "Be very careful how you hear." It's a dangerous thing to hear the Word of God, a dangerously marvelous thing.

Jesus explains in his parable that there once was a sower who went out to sow. Some of the seed that the farmer threw out landed on hard ground, and the seed could not penetrate the earth. Birds flew by and took the seed away. The hard ground, of course, represents the hard hearts of those who are unreceptive to the truth of God's Word. But nobody has to live with a calloused heart, because Jesus says there are other available responses to his Word.

The sower also sowed some seed in the midst of the rocks. In the ancient world of Israel, and in some cases even today, top soil was very thin. Limestone would peek through from underneath, and the seed could not effectively take root. The seed would go down a few inches and begin to sprout a plant, but as soon as the hot sun's rays shot down, the plant would wither and die. Jesus' point is that some people have a shallow heart—stony ground that can't maintain good growth. Perhaps they respond initially to the Word of God, but six months later they're nowhere to be found. They allowed the seed to get into the top layer of soil, but they kept the Word far from their soul.

The farmer threw still more seed onto the ground, where thistles and briars choked it out. The seed was overtaken by surrounding weeds, weeds that represent worldliness that stunts our growth still today. Whenever we allow our hearts to become distracted or divided by other interests, we lose our ability to be welcomers of the Word. And God won't force his way in.

But there is a fourth type of situation the farmer encountered as he spread his seed. Jesus says that there existed a certain amount of prepared soil, "good soil" that was ready to produce grain that would nourish life. Prepared soil—*this* is to be the reality of our lives.

X

When the Word of God gets planted deep inside of you, as the prophet Jeremiah said, it becomes your joy, the delight of your heart.[6] It becomes your oxygen, the most sustaining force in your life. It satisfies your deepest longings and the most profound needs in your life.

The Word of God is strength in our weakness. It is light in our dark night. It is medicine to heal the hurts of our lives. It is a shelter in the time of storm. It is a fortress when we face any enemy. It is the Truth that beats down every lie. It is the Book of books. It is the Book of Life. It is the *LifeBook*. And it is ours.

My prayer for us both is that daily we will share the apostle Peter's posture regarding where ultimate truth for living is found. "Lord, to whom shall we go? Only *you* have the words of eternal life."[7]

⋈

---

[6] See Jeremiah 15:16.

[7] See John 6:68, author's abridgment; emphasis added.

Please call 1-800-414-7693 or visit www.store-powerpoint.org to order the following products:

BOOKS:

A Man of God
Are you Fit for Life?
Courageous Parenting
Life According to Jesus
Lessons from the Heart
A Hope and a Future
Powering Up
Triumph! How You Can Overcome Death and Gain Eternal Life
A.S.K.: Unleashing the Power of Prayer

DEVOTIONALS:

Power for Daily Living
A Daily Encounter with God

BOOKLETS:

30 Days to Powerful Prayer
The Truth About Influence
True Womanhood
New Life in Christ
Rock Solid
Pause: Resting In God Instead of Stressing Out

GRAHAM
1-800-414-7693 (1-800-414-POWER)
jgraham@powerpoint.org
jackgraham.org